Only Connect

150 Prayers to Aid Reflection

Rupert Bristow

ONLY CONNECT
150 Prayers to Aid Reflection

Copyright © 2009 Rupert Bristow
Original edition published in English under the title ONLY CONNECT by
Kevin Mayhew Ltd, Buxhall, England.
This edition copyright © Fortress Press 2019

All rights reserved. Except for brief quotations in critical articles or reviews,
no part of this book may be reproduced in any manner without prior written
permission from the publisher. Email copyright@augsburgfortress.org or
write to Permissions, Fortress Press, PO Box 1209, Minneapolis, MN
55440-1209.

Cover image: Photo by YinYang on iStock
Cover design: Emily Wyland

Print ISBN: 978-1-5064-5937-0

Contents

Foreword	5
About the Author	6
Introduction	7

Contemplation

Relaxation	9
Reflection	12
Imagination	15
Meditation	18
Recuperation	22

Reconciliation

Mediation	25
Peacemaking	28
Conflict Resolution	31
Compromise	34
Negotiation	37

Exploration

Traveling	41
Risk-taking	44
Endurance	47
Launching Out	50
Looking Inward	53

Transformation

Life Changes	57
Marriage	60
Birth	63
Retirement	66
Illness and Disability	70

Transition

Conversion	73
Christening	76
Confirmation	79
Education	82
Employment	85

Consolation

Looking Back	89
Letting Go	93
Giving Thanks	96
Facing Doubt	99
Having Faith	102

Foreword

Prayer is the making of connections. We connect with those around us in the events of our lives, with the deep movements of our hearts and the desires and obsessions that drive us. And all of this we do through the great connection that God makes with us, and through which we are connected with every other living being.

The major challenge facing people of faith is how to help the world stay connected. We live in an age of fragmentation where individualism has been raised to the status of ideology. We're connected by the internet but not by the intricacies of relationship and community. We're connected by financial, economic, and political systems—often to our detriment—but not by the bonds of affection and respect on which our future depends. The cry goes up again: "Only connect!"

Rupert Bristow has written a book of connections. He connects us with the God of ridiculous generosity who calls us to wake up and come alive in the presence of his Son. He also connects us with the inner landscape we inhabit with all its risky journeys of exploration, transition, and transformation. Moreover, he keeps us rooted in the world of tarnished beauty, where to love God is to love God's creation, in all its complexity and ambivalence.

I very much hope that through these honest, searching, and inviting prayers we may find ourselves seeing the world more clearly through God's eyes, and loving all its parts and its people more mercifully and sacrificially. And I trust that this will start with our being more merciful to ourselves as we let ourselves go into the generous embrace of the living God. Rupert Bristow is a wise and compassionate guide and his book is a warm connection with a world of grace.

John Pritchard, Bishop of Oxford

For my wife, Sarah

About the Author

Rupert Bristow was Director of Education for Canterbury Diocese from 1995 until his retirement in 2008 and is active as a Reader in Trinity Benefice, Folkestone. He has worked in education—in schools, universities, and administration, at home and overseas—and has edited and written for various educational publications. He has chaired Kent SACRE (Standing Advisory Council for Religious Education) and is the author of *Prayers for Education* (Kevin Mayhew, 2008).

Introduction

The prayers in this volume are meant as aids to reflection on quite personal matters that often remain unexplored. I am not the first to use the E. M. Forster phrase, "Only connect," from *Howards End* as a title for a book, and won't be the last, but it summarizes perfectly what I attempt here.

If prayer is at the heart of a personal relationship with God, there are some parts of that relationship that can remain untouched by rushed daily prayer or intercessions squeezed into four minutes at a Sunday service. Of course there are prayers here that can be used to provide a focus on such occasions, but most are meant for where there is time to pray *and* listen to God.

The themes of contemplation, reconciliation, exploration, transformation, transition, and consolation may seem to be discrete subjects, but there is a unifying thread. That thread is one of active participation of mind, body, or spirit. Whether actively listening or traveling with a purpose, whether seeking to understand or precipitate change, or whether simply recognizing and marking a significant event or change in one's life, I hope these prayers will be of help to you.

I have been grateful for suggestions along the way as these prayers have taken shape, particularly those from my good friend, the Rev. Ben Tettey, who has kept pointing me back to the Lord's Prayer as the wellspring for all prayers.

Rupert Bristow

Contemplation

Relaxation

Lord,
it's been a busy time of late:
too much expected of me,
everything coming at once.
I need some peace.
Help me to relax—but not too much.
Bring me the peace that lasts—your peace:
the peace that frees the mind of worldly things,
the peace that brings us closer, Lord,
that opens my eyes and opens my heart,
that reconnects body and soul—as one.
Amen.

Refreshing God,
bring me a sense of proportion;
take my cares and transform them,
renew my stillness and help me to calm down,
and please remove my guilt at letting go.
May I relax into a proper enjoyment of your creation,
appreciate the purpose of being rather than doing,
and take time to put relationships before activity.
Let me be still and know that you are God.
Amen.

Lord of Life,
your Son wanted us to live life abundantly,
but I think I've been overdoing it recently.
Tell me how I can relax without fretting;
show me the way to value time and space.

Silence

Thank you for the gifts of silence and thought,
    rest, and relaxation.
Help me to be more myself in the company of friends,
and in my relationship with you.
Let me find time for relaxation without expectation,
as part of the abundance you have given us,
generous God.
Amen.

Lord of laughter and light,
bless this time of vacation and recreation.
By your grace we have this world to enjoy.
Help me to be a good steward of all that you have
    given us,
including the gifts of energy and rest.
As we start our vacation,
may our planning be sufficient without being
    prescriptive;
may we cast off worries but not responsibilities;
may we bring joy to others as well as ourselves;
may we have fun—and remember to thank you for it.
Amen.

Soothing Lord,
challenge me to slow things down.
Stop me from rushing about,
and draw me into a deep relaxation
when I hear you in the silence.

Silence

Help me to appreciate the time to think about you
    and me.
Let me grow in the love you have shown me,
and be open and responsive to the people I know
and the gifts they bring.
Amen.

Reflection

God of silence,
even in the noise of our lives,
feed my still center
as we glimpse the infinity of space and time.
Create in me a yearning heart
for the insights and understanding
of careful reflection,
and help me hold on to the fruits of reflection,
even where I am under pressure—especially when I am under pressure.
Thank you, Lord.
Amen.

Lord,
give me the ability to reflect deeply
on the things I see and the people I meet.
Help me to choose carefully the books I read
and the Bible passages I study.
When I feel angry at the words people use in print
or in person,
give me the capacity to reflect before I respond.
Let me think what Jesus would do and then pray about it.
Help me to pray naturally, not as a last resort.
In your mercy, Lord,
hear my prayer.
Amen.

Graceful God,
you have given us the power to think
   and the capacity to act,
the judgment to decide and the freedom to resist.
Pour down on us the example of your grace,
so that we may put everything in perspective,
seeking and showing generosity and trust,
even where it is not expected or deserved.
May our action reflect your thinking,
and our thinking reflect the example of your Son,
Jesus Christ.
Amen.

Wonderful Counselor,
be with me as I reflect on all that has happened today:
what I did . . .
why I did it . . .
what I have learned . . .
what I have given to others . . .
what others have given to me . . .
how I have shown my faith . . .
how I have shared my faith . . .
how I have honored your name . . .
what I will take into tomorrow . . .
what I will leave with you, Lord.
Thank you.
Amen.

Unfolding God,
lay bare my soul to your revelation,
and give me time and concentration in focusing on you
as I reflect on what has been and what might be.
Give me courage in facing the known,
foresight in anticipating the unexpected,
and creativity in my quiet time with you—
especially in my reflections on the daily reading
when it is often hard to make connections with my life.
Amen.

Imagination

Inspiring Lord,
let my imagination run free
to gasp at the wonder of your creation,
and to grasp at the thoughts and words
that will do it justice.
As I view the greens and browns and blues of nature,
as I hear the music of mankind,
help me to hold you in mind,
to honor the origins of all around me,
and to rekindle the relationship between God and man
in the imagination of my heart.
Through the one who is the source of our inspiration,
Jesus Christ.
Amen.

God of our imagination,
bring us the courage to think without limits,
to stretch our minds to take in the enormity
of the world, the universe and your Son.
We can see and touch and experience your world.
We can explore and admire and learn about your
    universe,
and, greatest of all, we know the love of your Son.
Through his ministry and sacrifice,
make us open to the Holy Spirit
in response to your grace and favor,
generous God.
Amen.

Extravagant Father,
we thank you that there is
so much more for us to learn,
so much more for us to see,
so much more for us to hear.
Bring me the energy and the vision to continue searching,
knowing that you are at the heart of everything
 in creation.
Protect us from the perils of not appreciating all that
 we come across,
and from the dangers of limiting our horizons,
 undervaluing your reach.
Guide us in our explorations
and inspire us to aim high in all that we do.
Through your trusting Son.
Amen.

CONTEMPLATION

Lord,
as I struggle to bring the words to match the moment
and the channel for expressing the fruit of the Spirit,
help me to pray . . .
for myself,
for my loved ones,
for my church,
for my work.
And, though I sometimes find it hard, Lord,
assist me to spend time and seek your inspiration
   to imagine the situation
of those in authority in our local and national
   government,
of the leaders of our Church,
of those in poverty and near death,
of the religious throughout the world who pray for us
   several times a day.
Imaginative God, help me to put myself in others' shoes
   as I pray for them.
Amen.

Lord of the spheres,
give us the imagination to dream your dreams
for the world, for our time, and for us.
You allow us the chance to break free from our past,
think new thoughts and put aside past deeds.
Help us to take risks for you
in our lives and in our hearts.
Let me be on the lookout for fresh ways to interpret
   your love
and new ways to express my faith.
Guide me in your great enterprise,
redeeming Lord.
Amen.

Meditation

At Break of Day

Lord of our lives,
help me to discern all that you are to me,
to glimpse the love that you have shown,
to understand your will in all that I do.

Silence

Lift my sights, Lord, when I worry about little things,
and let me learn to love those challenges you send.
Let me know your comfort in those things that trouble me.
Tell me how I can bring comfort to others.

Silence

I dedicate this day to you, listening Lord.
Amen.

In a Break at Work

God of faith and wonder,
be with me as I seek to make a difference in all that I do.
Help me to honor your name
in my dealings with other people and the way I behave.
Show me when and how to share my faith.
Let me meditate on the challenging parables
through which your Son taught us:
- the mustard seed;
- the buried treasure;
- the pearl of great price;
- the sower and the seed;
- the young lawyer;
- the prodigal son.

Now I'm ready to resume my other tasks of this day.
Thank you.
Amen.

In the Yard

God of nature and nurture,
as I stop and look at the plants and trees,
    the flowers and fruit,
let me admire your work.

Silence

Thank you for giving me the chance to work in your
    garden,
to share your creation,
to help build your kingdom.
Let me learn the lessons of tending this garden
    for the rest of my life.
This is so obviously a partnership between you and me,
    Lord.
How can I fail to see that everything in life
    is just the same, a shared effort,
as long as I realize that I am the junior partner,
your laborer in the vineyard?
Amen.

On Vacation

God of great adventures,
as you bring me new experiences on this vacation,
let me reflect on
    the scenery you have created,
    the people you have made in your own image,
    the cultures that distinguish as well as divide us,
    and the values that we share.
Let this vacation be our time of rest, knowing that you
    rested too, Lord,
and let us rejoice in it.
Amen.

At Bedtime

God of rest,
how did you and I do today?
Tell me what went well from your perspective.

Silence

Let me share what I did wrong.

Silence

What do I need to reflect on tonight?

Silence

Tell me what you expect of me tomorrow.

Silence

Thank you, Lord. That's a weight off my mind.
Can I sleep now?
Amen.

Recuperation

Healing Lord,
give my body time to mend.
Give my spirit hope to get well.
I have been aware of so many prayers.
Let those who have prayed know that you are listening.
I am so thankful, Lord, for the gifts you have given
to those who have cared for me:
doctors and nurses, family and friends, priests and laity.
Bring them comfort as you bring comfort
    in my recuperation.
All is well.
Amen.

Lord of wholeness,
you know how I feel.
I am recovering well.
Help me to rest some more,
even though I want to get on with things.
I find it hard to allow people to help.
I am so used to helping others,
but I am coming around to it.
People have such great gifts of goodwill
    and practical assistance.
Let that not surprise me.
I know it doesn't surprise you.
I pray this through your loving Son, Jesus Christ.
Amen.

Caring God,
be with N as *he/she* recovers from *his/her* operation.
Bless *him/her* with your presence and your comfort.
May all those around *him/her* be sensitive to *his/her* needs,
patient during convalescence,
and always mindful of the reality of your love.
We ask this in Jesus' name.
Amen.

Loving Lord,
let N's illness be followed by recovery that lasts.
Only you know what lies ahead.
Show us all the way to help bring healing and wholeness.
Above all, Lord, let N feel your comfort and presence
in the knowledge that you want the best for *him/her*,
as your Son always cared for those in need,
and still does.
Amen.

Father of all good things,
bring to those affected by the tragedy in N
a hope of recovery that is difficult to see just now,
as they grieve for the suffering around them,
as they mourn the dead and care for the living.
May the local community have the collective will,
    with your help, Lord,
to mend their brokenness
and bring new life out of the despair and grief of loss,
starting with the healing of the injured
and their restoration to the life you want them to lead.
Through your Son, the resurrected Lord.
Amen.

Reconciliation

Mediation

God of intervention,
you sent your Son to mediate in the world.
Inspire me to celebrate the fruits of that mediation
by learning your Son's ways,
by modeling his relationship with you
   and with mankind.
Let me appreciate and practice the true mediation
at work in the world, through our hearts.
You met us halfway through your Son.
The least I can do is reach out and grasp his hand.
Amen.

Lord of our relationships,
bring me judgment, wisdom, and humility
in the difficult relationship I have just now.
Let me not overreact, but seek common ground.
Point me toward your Son, who made all things new,
who gave us the opportunity for a right relationship
   with you,
for a new covenant that lasts beyond this life.
Bring perspective to my vision
and proportion to my actions.
Above all, Lord, let love hold sway over hate.
Through the one who overcame sin and death for us all,
Jesus Christ.
Amen.

God of reconciling love,
bring me patience in seeking to bring about peace.
It may be just between friends and family
    that mediation is necessary,
but I realize how this can spread to nations
where relationships are not right.
Please, Lord, let all concerned take a leaf out of your book
and draw back from actions they will regret—
    and you will not want.
Save them from themselves and help to play a part in
    mediating your will for them.
I ask this through Jesus, who wants the best for us all
    in your sight.
Amen.

Lord,
help our Church to resolve its internal problems
that threaten to split asunder the body of Christ
    you want us to be.
We know that you wanted us to serve you
    as your Son showed us,
and we know we have often failed miserably
    to do him justice.
Put aside our petty concerns and worries.
Make us strong for you, Lord, and not afraid of building
    bridges rather than widening cracks.
Let love for you take the place of love of ourselves,
through the one who put community before self,
    Jesus Christ.
Amen.

Listening Lord,
I lay before you the people who are having difficulty
  with each other just now.

Silence

I think that they are also having difficulty with you,
  gracious God.
Give them time to reflect on their relationship with you,
  I pray.

Silence

Hear their cry, Lord, and listen to these prayers.
May I do your will in all that you would wish for them.
Amen.

Peacemaking

Lord,
bring me peace in my heart
as I face this new day.
Let your calm be my strength
as I prepare for what lies ahead.
You have shown me how to trust in you;
you are my true friend.
Now help me to bring peace to those I meet,
so that they can know that perfect love
that you have shown through Jesus Christ.
Amen.

God of power and peace,
help me to build a bridge between those who don't listen
and those who choose not to hear.
There have been times, as you know, Lord,
when I didn't listen to you
or heed your call to me.
Now let me learn from my mistake
and bring hope to others as they struggle with their
    anger and their pride.
Let your peace break out and your love shine through.
We ask this through the grace of Jesus.
Amen.

Lord of righteousness,
watch over the groups in N
who are in conflict with each other.
You know the causes that they each have
and the strength of their feelings and their fears.
Bring a ray of hope to their dark, deep despair
and a breath of your Holy Spirit to their search for an
 end to the bloodshed.
Aid all those who are seeking resolution to the conflict
and bring a quiet determination to their actions,
steely God.
Amen.

Amazing God,
your power is boundless and restrained,
captured in creation—and in the stillness of deep waters.
We need that restraint just now in N.
May those who are fighting understand that they are
 desecrating your world
by their violence and selfishness.
Help them to know that it is not exercising superior
 power that shows true strength,
but the perseverance to seek peace that marks
 the wisdom of righteousness.
Help N in its hour of need through the example
 of your Son, Jesus Christ.
Amen.

United Godhead, Three in One,
how can you look on at your creation at war with itself?
May your combined power of Father, Son, and Holy
 Spirit
shake the perpetrators of these acts of violence
 into the realization
that they are wrong—and you are right.
Bring your tough love down on their heads,
and change their hearts and minds
to find time and space to make amends.
Sorry, Lord, for losing my temper.
Amen.

Conflict Resolution

Lord of might and right,
you used your power to show us your love
 through your Son.
Bring to the situation in N
that same willingness to develop a new covenant,
to renounce violence and force
and embrace a desire to break the cycle of destruction,
to build a lasting peace
and restore a right relationship with you,
through the peace of your Son, Jesus Christ.
Amen.

Heavenly Father,
you know the torment of struggle and loss
and also the peace that passes all understanding.
Help the warring factions in N today
to know that out of fear can come hope
if there is the will to see that there is a better way.
Let all thoughts of revenge and retaliation
give way to strength in seeking common ground.
May humanity replace brutality,
and resolve to end the conflict become the goal
 of all parties.
For the sake of the suffering of the innocent
and in Jesus' name.
Amen.

God of our times and all time,
help me to stop the escalation of conflict in our family.
I know I react very badly to provocation.
Especially, I pray, bring healing to my relationship
    with N.
Let me take the first steps to stop the strife
and may I be the first to admit fault if I have done wrong.
Please let your love into our lives so that we can be
    restored and renewed.
Through the love of your Son, Jesus Christ.
Amen.

Gracious God,
we need a bit of your grace just now.
The breakdowns in relationships at work are awful.
I don't know where to turn, other than to you.
I find it hard to keep out of the conflict and hurt,
but I want it all to stop.
Give me the courage, Lord, to take a stand
and help bring people together,
so that we can work as a team again.
Through your Son, who never wavered in his resolve,
    Jesus Christ.
Amen.

Insightful God,
I bring to you the conflicts inside me:
between discipline and indiscipline;
between selfishness and altruism;
between materialism and the spiritual;
between good and evil.
I pray especially today for the difficulties I have
in resolving the conflict over the issue of ...
How should I deal with this, Lord?
Give me the will and show me the way
so that I can truly find a lasting solution,
rather than a quick fix.
Through him who saved us for all time, Jesus Christ.
Amen.

Compromise

Lord,
I know that with you there is only one way,
but show me what that way should be for me,
especially if I am going in the wrong direction.
Bring me back to the right path, Lord,
and help me to understand the need to set my priorities
  to fit in with yours
and not the other way around!
Compromise my heart, but take my soul
and shape both to your purpose,
through the one who reconciled God and man,
  Jesus Christ.
Amen.

God of great understanding,
you know my strengths and weaknesses,
  my wants and needs.
In stillness, let me hear how you think I should balance
  the gifts you have given me.

Silence

I don't want to compromise or fail to use the talents
  you know I have,
but I know I can be selfish as well as single-minded.
May I blend the best of what I have to offer with the gifts
  of others
and give to you the credit for all I manage to achieve.
Let my life be the right sort of compromise between us—
a true partnership, with the help of your Son, Jesus Christ.
Amen.

Heavenly Father, Lord of all,
in the struggles and conflicts in the world,
may compromise be seen as strength, not weakness.
Let care for each person, made in your image,
be seen as the central issue, not as an afterthought.
Where there are seemingly irreconcilable difficulties,
especially in N,
bring insight and inspiration to the leaders
   in their search for a way forward.
May humility triumph over aggression,
and may passion for justice hold sway over desire
   for victory at all costs.
Lord, in your mercy, hear this prayer.
Amen.

Lord of worship and praise,
we sometimes don't know where to turn, except inward,
as we reflect on the issues in our church.
Challenge us to seek compromise without backing down
and understanding without selling out.
Open our eyes, Lord,
   to the possibilities and potential of your Church
rather than the deficiencies and defects.
Above all, give us the strength to move on
   from differences.
Compromise our will to the greater good of the work
   that needs to be done in the world—your work.
We ask this in the name of the one who is forever
   our partner and friend, your Son, Jesus Christ.
Amen.

God of surprising alliances,
we remind ourselves of your search for believers
 among the forgotten, the failed, and the fallen:
how you were supported and followed by fishermen,
 bartenders, and sinners;
how you ministered to the poor and needy—
 and healed the sick.
Let us not compromise our principles to gain access
 to the great and the good,
but be true to ourselves and how you want us to be
by seeking a true compromise, a creative reconciliation
between our needs as humans and your expectations
 as our God.
Only with the help of your Son, Jesus Christ.
Amen.

Negotiation

God of dialogue and relationship,
help me to create the right atmosphere
for discussion, constructive argument, and lasting
 agreement.
You and I know it won't be easy,
but together we can get there.
Bring me strength.
Bring me wisdom.
Bring me insight.
Thank you, Lord.
Amen.

Lord of tough love,
create in us the will to resolve our difficulties,
to negotiate instead of grandstand,
to make proposals that are realistic,
to give proper consideration to different approaches
and, more than anything, Lord, to listen to you
 and discern your will.
We pray for a solution that will last and one that we can
 all own,
including you, Creator God.
Amen.

Lord of all,
we pray for the trouble spots of the world today,
in particular N,
where negotiations are currently taking place.
May all the parties involved enter these in good faith,
resolved to find a way forward rather than looking
    for new stumbling blocks.
Inspire the leaders with insight and vision,
so that good can come out of brokenness,
as your Son, Jesus Christ, would want.
Amen.

Heavenly Father,
look upon our family with favor and forgiveness.
We know that there have been tensions and tough
    words said.
Help us to discuss, listen, and negotiate our way to
    peace in the household.
We try to keep your commandments, but sometimes
    slip up
in properly honoring you and each other.
If we can get our relationship right with you,
there is nothing that can stop us from sorting this out.
Through the one who knew the difficulties
    of family life,
your Son, our Savior, Jesus Christ.
Amen.

God of the future,
let those who negotiate for reductions in our
    wastefulness know your will.
Reveal to us the real dangers of our impact on your
    world.
We pray especially for those involved in negotiations on:
trade . . .
environmental policies . . .
arms control . . .
nuclear proliferation . . .
climate change.
Bring to us all a better understanding of good stewardship
    in our part of your universe.
Amen.

Exploration

Traveling

Lord of all journeys,
be with me as I travel,
as your world is revealed to me,
as your diversity is impressed upon me,
as I see your presence all around me.
Help me to be open and receptive, appreciative
　　and trusting.
Trust me to be helpful to those around me.
Make me wary of those who may do me harm,
but grateful to those who wish me well.
What a world you have made!
Thank you for showing me and sharing a part of it.
Through your Son who made the ultimate journey,
our Lord, Jesus Christ.
Amen.

God of great destinations,
we are a pilgrim people.
Give us a goal to achieve, a place to aim for,
but bring to us a real appreciation of the journey
  along your way,
wherever that takes us, whoever we meet.
Let us relish every moment as we accompany you,
every person we encounter in your name,
each mountain and river, village and city.
Help us to spread our wings, look as far and wide
  as we can,
and bring us safely home.
We ask this in Jesus' name.
Amen.

Heavenly Father, who leads us and follows us,
watch over our journey and our fellow travelers
as we set off with excitement and expectation.
You have been with us in our planning and in our
  preparation.
May we be always grateful that you will be with us
  in our journeying.
Help us to recall all we have read and all we have
  learned,
so that we can do full justice to the places we go
and bring back memories of experiences we can draw on
  when we come home.
We ask this through your Son, our guide, Jesus Christ.
Amen.

God of going out,
we pray for those who are travelling soon,
especially N as they go to N.
Keep them from harm,
but put in their way all that interests and surprises
    about your world,
so that they can learn from those who give them
    hospitality.
May their trip be a pilgrimage of hope and enjoyment,
a journey of fun and fascination,
and may they share their experiences with us
    when they return,
as your Son will.
Amen.

Lord without limits,
thank you for helping us to explore the boundaries
    of your creation
through reading, listening, looking, and learning,
as well as through traveling;
for preparing us before we journeyed;
for being present as we went;
and for being with us in our homecoming.
Spend time with us now as we reflect in silence
    on all we have learned . . .
from the places we went . . .
from the people we met . . .
from the things we did . . .
and from your presence with us now.
We give thanks for the boundless love you have shown
    through your Son, Jesus Christ.
Amen.

Risk-taking

Lord,
you took the biggest risk of all
by sending your Son to bring us back to you.
Help me to take risks as I explore your world,
knowing that you are there to watch over me.
Give me energy and inspiration
as I attempt things I never thought I would do,
as I challenge myself and those around me.
Let me trust and be trusted,
as there is only so much I can do alone.
And may I always trust in you,
ever-present and ever-ready God.
Amen.

God of change and continuity,
make me push back the boundaries of my experience
and extend the limits of my horizons.
No place is strange to you, creator of all,
so why should anything in the world be strange to me?
Thank you for the many ways I can explore this richness
and the means to record and recall all that happens
    as I do so.
But let me savor the moment of discovery of new things,
rather than add them to my list of things achieved;
and especially, Lord, help me to make new friends
    wherever I go.
I ask this through Jesus Christ.
Amen.

Reassuring Lord,
give me strength to be tough when I need to be.
As I enter new territory in every sense,
let me remember the way you provided for your people
   in the desert.
You have always been faithful to pilgrims down the ages,
giving purpose and vision to travelers in their coming
   and going.
As I set out on my journey to N,
open my eyes to new people and places,
to new sights and sounds,
and to creatures I have never encountered.
Keep me safe, keep me healthy,
and keep me searching for your kingdom,
loving Lord.
Amen.

God of letting go,
let's make this risk assessment together
as we pray for what's ahead:
the risk of staying in our safety zone . . .
the risk of not asking questions . . .
the risk of worrying too much . . .
the risk of forgetting your presence . . .
the risk of looking back or forward and not enjoying
   the moment.
Thank you, Lord, for helping us to sort out what is
   important
as we seek to live life in all its abundance.
Through your Son, Jesus Christ.
Amen.

Liberating Lord,
we pray, as your Son taught us, for our daily bread.
Make it essential in all our exploration of your world
that we do everything in our power—and yours,
to bring this about, not just for ourselves, not just for
 today,
but for everyone and for all time.
Bring growing awareness, capacity, and commitment,
 as we journey,
to make a difference and a Christian statement
that your will needs to be done,
in this world and the next.
And that it is only through sharing the bread of life
that we are one body, uniting God.
Amen.

Endurance

Long-suffering Lord,
teach me the art of endurance:
how the hard road is often the right route.
I am often tempted to take shortcuts,
even when I know in my heart that I shouldn't.
Give me the stamina for the long haul,
the vision for the long term,
and the energy to sustain both.
Knowing that you are always there for me,
I put my trust in you.
Amen.

Almighty God,
you made us in your image,
but we often let you down.
Give us the perseverance and the commitment to carry on,
even when everything seems to be against us.
Your Son taught us to pray to you
and suffered for us, even to death.
Help us, Lord, to live up to his example;
to be a living sacrifice in all we do,
to continue in his way against all obstacles,
to go the long way around if the alternative is to be
  without you.
Through the one who endured everything for us,
  Jesus Christ.
Amen.

Heavenly Father,
our endurance is tested every day
in our duty to you, as we watch and pray.
But we crave the perfect freedom that lies in serving you.
Put our faith journey first in our lives,
so that it can take us where you want,
so that our personal and family life can be underpinned
　in faith.
You are there for the long haul,
and we need to reflect that day by day—
by carrying out your tasks,
by advancing your kingdom, at home and abroad,
by understanding the interdependence of your creation,
and by standing firm in the name of Jesus Christ,
　　our Lord.
Amen.

Lord of new things,
make us persistent and prepared,
as well as excited and spontaneous,
in our exploration of your world.
Give us endurance alongside the desire to experience
　new places,
so that we may appreciate and understand
　all that has gone before.
We know we are fortunate to benefit from our
　forebears,
so let us leave a lasting legacy
by doing justice to their achievements,
showing respect in our interpretation,
and building patiently on all their work—and yours, Lord.
Amen.

Lasting Lord,
let me reflect on the endurance of your Son . . .
in his healing . . .
in his teaching . . .
in his response to accusation . . .
in the face of betrayal . . .
in his suffering on the cross . . .
in carrying out his Father's will.
Help to build up my endurance to complete your tasks
    for me in my faith journey, especially at this time.
Remembering always your Son's endurance
    for my sake.
Amen.

Launching Out

Heavenly Father,
this is the first time I have traveled by air.
Thank you for the opportunity to survey your creation
 from above.
Take away my fear of flying,
especially the taking off and landing.
You have given us the ability and means to fly,
to help us explore all the elements in your world.
I pray that the confidence and training of the crew
may make this a memorable experience
and a sign of your high expectations for us all,
made in your image, and saved by your Son, Jesus Christ.
Amen.

Lord of the air,
as we take off and rise up,
let my spirits leap too
at the opportunities ahead.
It is always your wish that we live life to the full,
and we wonder at all that you have provided,
both the means by which we can stretch our horizons
and the sheer range and variety of your creation
 that we see.
Let us be safe and secure in the knowledge that,
 even up here,
you guide us and journey with us, our true navigator.
Amen.

Lord of all continents,
as we explore areas new to us,
we turn to you, for whom nothing is new.
Help us to adapt and be open,
to be receptive and aware,
so that the experience will be one from which we
    can learn and grow.
I look forward especially, Lord, to . . .
And while I am abroad, please watch over those I leave
    behind, especially N.
Knowing that life goes on wherever you are present,
we ask this through your Son, Jesus Christ.
Amen.

Heavenly Father,
lord of sea and sky, land and lake,
create in me a searching soul,
a desire to find out what lies above and beneath sea level.
Thank you for the gift of travel,
by road, rail, air, sea, or ski.
Let me never be restricted by fear in exploring
    your world,
but let me also be properly prepared,
    practically and spiritually,
for the journeys that I make,
including the last one home, to you,
God of going out and coming in.
Amen.

Almighty God,
who made the oceans greater than the land,
who held the seas back for Moses,
who provided fish to feed mankind,
let our voyage be one where the seas are kind to us,
and the winds are right for our trip.
Let us be aware of what lies beneath the waves,
and how storms can suddenly develop on the surface.
Keep this ship safe on its course,
and may it open up the world
to our exploration and your beneficence.
Amen.

Looking Inward

Lord of inner strength,
you showed, through your Son, the power of faith.
Bring me to understand and feel that strength
in the way I face difficulty and disappointment,
and in the way I deal with the despair of others.
You have been gracious to me, Lord, in the good times,
when I probably did not thank you enough.
Let your light pierce my soul
and bring awareness of our relationship in its fullness,
forgiving God.
Amen.

Heavenly Father,
with your help, let me examine the state of my faith
   today.
When do I turn to you?
Why do I turn to you?
When do I really worship you?
When do I share my faith?
What are the doubts I have?
Please, Lord, show me how I can deepen my faith—
and share it with others.
Through the love and example of your Son, Jesus Christ.
Amen.

Mighty Counselor,
turn me inside out and upside down,
if it means I can know you better.
As I look deeply into my soul,
I sometimes feel there is nothing there,
and no real desire to grow in faith.
Let me feel something of the fervor of the first disciples.
Open up the insights of the early Fathers
and create the hunger in me
to learn to love you more and more each day.
Through your Son, my tutor, Jesus Christ.
Amen.

God the giver,
make us want to explore our faith journeys
in all our church activities and daily devotions.
We are often praying for people far away,
but do we realize they may be praying for us?
We pray for the poor and suffering in the world,
but please direct us in how we should respond
  in other ways.
Bring to us a realization that the poor and the suffering
may be praying about our indifference, our poverty
  of spirit, our turning away from you.
Create in us an understanding of the gifts and gaps
  in our lives
and how we can draw on your guidance to get a better
  balance.
Amen.

Amazing Lord,
as I seek to explore your ways,
may I do so with true humility,
rather than assuming that all I have to do is listen.
I realize I must work at my faith
and put in the hard yards, alongside the flashes of insight.
Point me to the books of those who have struggled
   with these issues,
even those I find difficult at times,
like Paul and N.
Make me read or listen to someone I don't really
   understand or agree with,
but who may have a lot to teach me.
Help me to be open to new ideas
and push me up that steep learning curve
to a better understanding of you,
immanent God.
Amen.

Transformation

Life Changes

Eternal God,
you are Lord of change and changelessness.
Bring me insight and understanding
as the milestones of life are reached:
my own and of those around me.
Let me savor and appreciate each one,
knowing that you are with me all the way.
From the miracle of birth to the mystery of death,
each step is into new territory for me,
but not for you, whose Son broke the barriers of sin
    and death for all time
and shares my joy and pain.
I ask this in Jesus' name.
Amen.

Understanding Lord,
create in me the capacity to cope with change,
to realize the potential you have given me
    at every stage of my life,
never thinking that I can do it all myself
or that everything will go smoothly.
But listening to others and to you along the way,
I know that some changes will be expected and planned,
while others will hit me suddenly and hard.
Let my preparation be in building the capacity to respond,
not in the acquisition of material things
    for all eventualities.
Help me to heed warning signs,
as well as look for encouraging ones,
and may curiosity for what lies ahead
outweigh any fear of the unknown.
Through the one who changed us all,
your Son, Jesus Christ.
Amen.

Heavenly Father,
who gave us night and day, sun and moon,
who brought us summer and winter, spring and autumn,
let us celebrate change and transformation—
the natural order of things.
Just as you created change,
so let us appreciate the continuity too.
We thank you, Lord, that your Church marks every
    change—
from christening to confirmation, from weddings
    to funerals—
while staying a symbol of your presence in the world,
an evolving witness to the ministry of your Son,
    our Savior, Jesus Christ.
Amen.

Constant Lord,
forgive us our need for your attention,
especially when we are facing changes or encountering
 difficulty.
It's just that life changes often come in your time, not ours,
even when you surprise us,
because it reminds us that we are human and you are God,
though it can be inconvenient.
You and I know that progress is not as certain as change,
but please don't remind us of that too often.
Thank you, Lord.
Amen.

Transforming God,
keep me open to your Holy Spirit,
so that I can do what you really want of me.
It would be so easy for me to shut up shop,
to refuse to budge from my ways
rather than seek your way.
So often I take the soft option,
when you want me to make the hard choice.
I need your support and direction, Lord,
so that when the big changes come
I can cope with the implications
for me and those around me.
Give me the capacity to change and be changed
through your Son, Jesus Christ.
Amen.

Marriage

Lord God,
you created man and woman
to tend your world and each other.
Help us to be true to your vision
in the way we love,
in the way we take joint responsibility,
in the way we care for each other,
in the way we nurture children,
in the way we worship you,
and in the way we honor and cherish our own parents,
knowing that you remain Father of all,
including your Son, Jesus Christ.
Amen.

Heavenly Father,
bless our friends N and N
as they take their vows before you.
May they come to love you more
   as they grow in their love for each other.
Grace their union with the blessing of children
   if it is your will,
and may their home be a source of comfort
   and hospitality for family and friends.
In their life together, let each flourish—
   and may they jointly prosper,
sharing the gift of marriage and the blessing
   of companionship,
through the love of your Son, Jesus Christ.
Amen.

Lord of life and love,
on the wedding day of N and N,
shine your blessings on their lives
and warm their hearts in love.
May they draw on the best experiences of growing up
as they prepare for parenthood,
and may they know the love of each other's parents
as they create a home for themselves,
sharing hospitality and being good neighbors
as you would want them to be.
Amen.

Lord,
help us to mend our breaking marriage.
Open our hearts to each other—and to you.
It has been tough for us both recently.
Let us reflect on what has gone wrong . . .
Put into our minds and hearts how we can make it work,
what I should do,
what we should do.
Please, Lord, let us try harder to remember our vows
   made before you, and stick to them
out of a wish to do so, not out of fear of doing wrong.
Rekindle our love, redeeming Lord.
Amen.

Gracious God,
we commend to you all who embark on married life,
knowing that it is your will that unions between men
    and women should be blessed in your name.
As your Son was a wedding guest in Cana,
so may he be a frequent visitor
    in marriages and families known to us,
welcomed in and honored at times of celebration,
comforting and consoling in times of despair and loss,
caring and healing when sickness strikes,
and inspiring and nurturing in the knowledge and love
    of you,
so that you are known as a friend of the family,
Father of all.
Amen.

Birth

Father God, who makes all things new,
we ask for your blessing on this birth;
that this act of creation will transform our lives
 and all that we are,
knowing we have new responsibilities,
alongside new joys and explorations.
May our baby be your child, too, Lord,
and may *he/she* come to know and love you.
Protect *him/her* as *he/she* makes *his/her* way in life,
and let our nurturing do justice
to the world that this new soul has entered.
Through the Son whose birth was a new beginning
 for us all,
Jesus Christ.
Amen.

Loving Lord,
the hour is come for new life to emerge
in the miracle that is a newborn child.
You watched as your Son was born in Bethlehem,
that first Christmas when the world changed.
May this baby be welcomed and cherished,
and brought up with the selfless love
that Mary and Joseph showed all those years ago.
Strengthen us to do our very best
to take our fair share of responsibility
while entrusting *him/her* to your special care
as *he/she* grows in faith, with the help of godparents
 and the wider church family,
your family, Lord.
Amen.

God of beauty,
thank you for the safe birth of N,
for parents N and N,
and for all the medical, nursing, and midwifery staff
    involved.
Let the celebration be joined in heaven
by all those who went before,
and whose memory means so much to us today.
Ring out bells of hope
and chimes of freedom
for the new generation.
Create in us the right response
to a baby's cry and a sweet smile
that spells out transformation.
We ask this in Jesus' name.
Amen.

Almighty God,
help all those who struggle to give birth,
those who have tried and not been able to conceive,
those who have lost their baby naturally,
and those who have had a termination.
We bring to you also, Lord,
the mothers who, through poverty and starvation,
have been unable to sustain the life of infants,
and through disease and disorder
have seen the lives of offspring ebb away.
We thank you for the gift of life.
We know that everyone is precious in your sight,
whether their lives are short or long,
    deprived or well provided for,
loving Lord.
Amen.

Lord,
let the miracle of birth be a beacon of hope.
Bring to us an awareness of the potential of the new
in the transformation that is the creation of life.
Let us reflect on what birth can mean
to us,
to mothers,
to fathers,
to you.
And let us rejoice in the force for good
   that family life can be
if you are at the heart of it.
Through the Son whose birth brought you joy,
Jesus Christ.
Amen.

Retirement

Lord of rest and peace,
I am not used to this new way of life.
Help me to see the potential of it all.
You have been with me during my working years,
steered me through my career,
with all its ups and downs.
Be with me now in the choices I make,
in the way we relate at home,
and in the new tasks that await me.
Thank you for helping me to be useful in your world.
May I find time to work in your service, more and more,
through the one whose service is perfect freedom,
    Jesus Christ.
Amen.

Heavenly Father,
let me pause and reflect on this milestone of retirement.
To me it is strange and new,
especially after all the nice things people said
   when I stepped down.
What awaits me now?

Silence

What do you wish me to do, Lord?

Silence

And the family?

Silence

Are there gifts that I have that could be of help
   to your Church?
Please make known your call as I pray to discern your
   will for me.

Silence

I ask this in Jesus' name.
Amen.

Redeeming and forgiving God,
as I retire from one episode of my life,
I realize that I was led and influenced by the world
   too much,
striving to do rather than be,
seeking to impress more than to support and inspire,
not letting you into my life—
except where things went wrong.
So forgive me for not thanking you enough,
and let me now know you better
through daily prayer and reflection
and through listening carefully to what others say,
both in the church and in the wider community,
not forgetting the family and neighbors I have neglected.
I ask this through your Son, who gave us a second chance,
Jesus Christ.
Amen.

Almighty God,
we pray for all retired people at this time:
for the enterprises that will continue to flourish
   because of their contribution;
for the work friends they left behind;
for the love and challenge you gave to them
   and expected of them;
and, most of all, Lord, for their future work in your
   vineyard.
May they be open-minded and generous with their time
   and skills;
may they experience aspects of your world that are new
   to them;
and may they grow in the love and knowledge of you
   on their journey home.
Through Jesus Christ, our Lord.
Amen.

God of mystery,
let retirement be an opportunity for exploration,
not a winding down of curiosity.
May we be a continuing learning community,
whatever our age or stage in life.
But in celebrating the freedom of retirement,
let us be aware of those who are suddenly alone,
those who do not have the means to take advantage
 of their retirement,
those who find it difficult to adjust to life changes,
and those whose children do not seem to be interested
 in them.
How can we make retirement fun, Lord,
for us and for all those we have more time for?
Keep us up to the mark so that we can truly love others
 as we love ourselves.
We ask this knowing that you never rest, retire, or give
 up on us, eternal Father.
Amen.

Illness and Disability

Healing Lord,
lay your hands on me as I fight this illness.
Calm me and let the treatment take its course.
Help me to trust those who minister to me,
and be with them, Lord, in all that they do.
May those affected by my illness—
at home, at work, at church—
be reassured that you are present in my healing,
and let restoration to full health
be my aim and your will,
through your Holy Spirit.
Amen.

God of power and might,
let the harm and hurt inside me be cast out,
so that I can once again hold my head up high.
Bring back the positive me
that always ran the course,
that never held back,
that saw the potential of anything
    rather than the drawbacks of everything.
At the same time, I know that time can be a healer,
and that I cannot expect too much too quickly.
So, loving Lord, bring me patience to trust your timescale
and faith that I will get well.
Through your Son, the healer.
Amen.

Heavenly Father,
help me to bear the pain of this illness,
which the experts say is chronic.
You and I have come through a lot together,
so let us tackle this in the same way.
I'll tell you how it feels today ...

Silence

Now let me know how you can help,

Silence

and what you need me to do.

Silence

I am aware of so many prayers being said for me.
Help me to feel the power of that prayer.
Thank you, Lord.
Amen.

God of gifts and challenges,
you have enabled me to cope with my disability.
Please help others to do so too.
I give thanks that I can access so many things now.
Give me the courage to push back the boundaries further,
to attempt more than I can reasonably expect to do
because you, Lord, through your Son,
made everything possible, made all things new.
Create in us all the yearning to find new things we can do,
but only with your help, God of grace and generosity.
Amen.

Almighty God,
who gives to each of us certain gifts and strengths,
help us to make the most of all that we are,
so that we can be the person you want us to be.
Let us learn lessons and seek inspiration
from those who, despite age and disability,
remain cheerful and faithful in all that they do.
Let them be an example to us
and a witness to your presence in our lives.
Be with us, Lord, in the dark times,
but let us also acknowledge your love in the good times.
And finally, Lord, may it be as good to arrive
   as to travel in hope.
We ask this in the assurance of salvation,
through Jesus Christ, our Lord.
Amen.

Transition

Conversion

Lord,
I have only just met you.
I want to know all about you.
Friends have spoken of the difference you have made
    to their lives,
and I have begun to study the Bible.
Your Son's words and miracles are a revelation to me.
He seems to speak directly to me when he addresses
    the disciples—
and to think he died to save me from all my wrongdoings!
Your forgiveness is so important if I am to make
    progress in my faith.
Help me to learn quickly and love openly,
through the one who has given me new life,
your Son, Jesus Christ.
Amen.

God of infinite grace and mercy,
I pray that the good news that has reached N
will grow and develop *his/her* newfound faith.
May all of us play a part in grounding *his/her* enthusiasm.
Inspire us, Lord, in our support,
and bring new insights for us along the way.
I sense in *him/her* the excitement that the first disciples
    must have felt
and realize too the pressures that are to be faced,
remembering the brittleness of the witness of the apostles
when faced with challenges that came thick and fast.
Help us to provide the fertile soil
that can make strong roots for a faith that lasts,
through the one who taught us so much
    and gave us his all,
Jesus Christ.
Amen.

Almighty God,
you sent your Son to create a new covenant
when mankind had lost its way.
May your saving grace shine out anew,
so that those who still do not know your name
come to recognize that you are God.
Let the Bible speak out to them,
let questions be asked and answered,
and may the gift of prayer be offered and received.
Above all, Lord, may the richness of your creation
be acknowledged in our praise and worship,
and your love felt by new people every day.
We ask this through your Son, Jesus Christ.
Amen.

Transforming God,
we give thanks for those who bring others to faith,
whether by what they say or what they do,
by quiet witness or inspired by the Holy Spirit.
We remember especially the early missionaries
   to this country,
as well as the missionaries who have gone out
   from this country.
Today you have blessed your Church with mission
   partners
who work alongside churches at home and abroad,
strengthening mission and bringing fresh insights.
May their work prosper and may we be refreshed
   and encouraged
in sharing your word and seeking new Christians,
with the help of your Son, Jesus Christ.
Amen.

Amazing Lord,
we should never put limits on your reach,
or restraints on your domain,
so bring us the strength and the means to do your will.
Give us the courage to speak in your name,
to be true to your word
and to be empowered by the Holy Spirit
to share the good news.
May the memory of all those who have gone before—
disciples, martyrs, evangelists, and those who did small
   acts of Christian love for us—
inspire us to follow your Son's example of servanthood,
through Jesus Christ, our Lord.
Amen.

Christening

Dear Lord,
please welcome N to your Church today.
With water your Son was baptized by John.
With water N is made a member of our congregation.
May all in the family and the church family celebrate
    this special day:
special for N,
special for *his/her* parents,
special for *his/her* godparents,
and special for you, loving Father,
as the continuity of your kingdom
takes another step forward,
another opportunity for Christian hope,
another blessing, through your Son, our Savior,
Jesus Christ.
Amen.

Heavenly Father,
we are taking this step for N
knowing that you want to welcome *him/her*
    to your Church.
Help us to be good parents and wise counselors.
Let the light of Christ shine in N's life,
and whatever challenges *he/she* may face,
we pray that you are always alongside,
ready to lift and protect, as well as encourage and enable.
Thank you for the next phase in *his/her* life,
which we celebrate in Jesus' name.
Amen.

God of new beginnings,
I ask that this step I am taking to be baptized
is one that you wish me to take.
It is not easy for me, at my age,
to seek to make up for lost time.
But I really want to be a full member of your Church,
to be blessed with water in the name of Father, Son,
 and Holy Spirit,
to experience even more closely the love
 that you have already shown,
the compassion that I feel as I get to know your Son.
Help me through this transition and strengthen me
 in the faith,
through Jesus Christ.
Amen.

Almighty God,
our church today rejoices in celebration,
as *N* is welcomed as a pilgrim on the
 Christian way.
May the water and the sign of the cross
mark the start of *N's* journey,
and may the light of Christ illuminate *his/her* path,
so that as *he/she* takes *his/her* first steps and grows in
 strength and independence,
he/she may feel your love grow into faith that lasts.
We ask this through Jesus Christ, our Lord.
Amen.

Gracious Lord,
let me take very seriously the task of being a godparent,
knowing that I have been entrusted with important
 responsibilities.
Help me to recall the ways in which my godparent(s)
 assisted me,
and let me remember how I felt about it.
More than anything, Lord, let me do your will in all
 I attempt,
and may *N's* spiritual well-being be a prime focus.
If I can show a fraction of your Son's love for me,
I'll be doing a good job.
Through the one who shows us the way, now and always,
Jesus Christ.
Amen.

Confirmation

Entrusting God,
you received me at my baptism,
and gave responsibility to my parents and godparents
to bring me up in the faith of Christ.
Now I want to take my own step on that journey
as I seek your blessing on my confirmation.
In all this you have been my compass and my shield.
As I travel further on your path,
let me be always open to the Holy Spirit
and ready to play a full part in our Christian
 community.
We ask this in Jesus' name.
Amen.

Lord of spirit and grace,
come down on N today.
Release and confirm *him/her* in *his/her* faith,
so that *he/she* may grow in the love of your Son
and make that personal connection with you
that will last throughout this life and into the next.
In silence and in confidence we pray for N
and all others being confirmed today.
Knowing that you listen to our prayers
 and see into our hearts,
come close through your Son, Jesus Christ.
Amen.

God our guide and our compass,
as N confirms *his/her* Christian commitment,
let us all—family and friends, parents and godparents—
support and encourage *him/her* on the path your Son
    taught us,
whatever the temptations to stray.
Bring purpose to *his/her* life
and a willingness and burning desire
to know you better and make you better known,
through the love of your Son, Jesus Christ.
Amen.

God of growth,
today is all about sharing the light of Christ
as N takes the next step in faith.
Illuminate the way and shine even in dark corners,
so that *he/she* can be a witness to the love
    that you have bestowed.
We give thanks for the job of godparents,
who are always there to bring a special contribution,
encouraging the nurturing of *his/her* spiritual side.
In the midst of everything else expected nowadays,
bring a sacred space to *his/her* heart
and a love of community to *his/her* worship,
through the one who shared everything, Jesus Christ.
Amen.

Almighty God,
you have given us the gift of life.
You have also provided us with insight and free will
to make up our minds and develop our beliefs.
Assist the transition that those who are being confirmed
   are making.
It is just one step along the way,
but a big one, Lord.
Just as you have been with people in their first,
   faltering steps of faith,
enveloped in the love that baptism brought,
so now protect and grow their faith
in order to bring you nearer.
Thank you, Lord.
Amen.

Education

God of growth and wisdom,
as our child N starts school,
watch over *him/her* as *he/she* finds *his/her* feet.
Bring a sense of community to all that happens at school.
Bring a sense of interdependence in the relationships there,
and bring a love of learning to all they do.
As *he/she* explores the wonders of your world,
help *him/her* to understand that every child
   matters to God,
who has shown his love through Jesus Christ.
Amen.

Lord of challenge,
be with N as *he/she* starts middle school.
Bring resilience to the way *he/she* handles new things
   and new people.
Help *him/her* to put into practice those ways of working
   learned at elementary school,
confidently making new friends
   and finding *his/her* way around the new school.
When Jesus is not regarded as cool,
let *him/her* be strengthened in faith.
When Christianity is ignored or ridiculed,
let the examples in the Bible come to mind—
where it was Jesus who stood fast
and mockers who had to eat their words.
Above all, Lord, let faith grow from within,
alongside the joy of knowledge and love of learning,
through your Son, the teacher, Jesus Christ.
Amen.

All-knowing God,
the time for choice about *college* is here.
Help me to look at the right things as I start the process.
Make me open to hear all that parents and friends say,
but let me also listen to your voice in that choice.

Silence

Give me discernment in my research,
let me be confident in my application,
and let me learn from success and failure in all that I do,
so that I can be the person you want me to be.
I ask this in Jesus' name.
Amen.

Lord of all, shepherd of the sheep,
we pray for our *son/daughter*
as *he/she* starts at *University/College*.
We are so proud and yet so anxious.
Take away our fears but not our concerns.
Banish our worries but not our interest,
as *he/she* makes *his/her* way in the next chapter
   in *his/her* life.
May the high expectations we have for what *he/she*
   might achieve
be always moderated by unconditional love
as we remember the grace you show without condition,
through the love of your Son, Jesus Christ.
Amen.

God of achievement and purpose,
I could not have achieved this qualification without you:
without your power that created the world;
without your love through family and friends;
without your presence when things got tough,
and without that spark of inquiry
    that you have always encouraged.
So let me move on to my next challenge,
confident in myself,
confident in you,
and confident that I can make a difference in your world,
through the love and example of your Son, Jesus Christ.
Amen.

Employment

Heavenly Father,
you asked your disciples to make huge changes
when you invited them to follow you.
What task do you have for me
   as I think about the next step?

Silence

My qualifications are important as means,
but what are the ends you have in mind?

Silence

With my work life ahead of me,
I want to make the right choices
and give the right weight to each factor.
Please keep my mind open and my heart engaged,
but most of all, Lord, I want to heed your call.
I ask this in Jesus' name.
Amen.

Lord of high endeavor,
help me in my efforts at work at this time
as I take on more and more responsibility,
and expectations rise about my ability to deliver.
You have given me gifts that have held me in good stead,
talents that I hope you feel I have developed and used.
Let me get the right balance between work and home,
so that loved ones feel loved
and work colleagues feel supported.
May the confidence you have given me
survive any test and challenge ahead,
through the inspiration of your Son, Jesus Christ.
Amen.

God who gives and takes away,
you know what it is to suffer loss.
Let us pray for those who have lost their jobs recently,
especially ...
Be close to those most affected, Lord:
the families,
the community,
the friends.
May neighbors watch over their welfare
and support services be sensitive to their needs,
so that new opportunities are offered and grasped
in the knowledge of the love of your Son, Jesus Christ.
Amen.

Almighty God,
let us not forget the impact of our economy
on the employment of our brothers and sisters
    in other countries.
Help us to buy fairly and trade fairly,
so that there is just reward for work done well,
and long-term hope for whole communities
rather than short-term gain for international companies.
We ask, Lord, that there is gradual transition
from inequality to equality in the world
and from unjust to just systems,
so that the gifts and labors of all
are properly rewarded and duly honored.
We ask this through the one we honor and serve—
Jesus Christ.
Amen.

God of great expectations,
may we aim high in all we do,
volunteer where we can make a difference,
bring on the talents of others we know,
and treat our colleagues fairly.
Especially, Lord, we pray for a sure touch
   as we cope with change,
knowing that some people can handle this better
   than others.
Give me the strength not to take the easy way
if the hard way is the correct course,
and let me never forget to acknowledge the efforts
   of others
as partners in the process of change and development,
recognizing the model of your Son,
who sent out the seventy-two
to do his work and spread your word.
Through the one who fulfilled your expectations,
and always exceeds ours,
Jesus Christ.
Amen.

Consolation

Looking Back

God of past and present,
thank you for the memories of N,
which help me to bear the loss
and bring fond recollections
of things we've done together:
of special days,
of difficulties shared,
of special celebrations,
of journeys made,
of destinations reached.
May they always remain until we meet again.
In the promise of your kingdom,
through your Son, Jesus Christ.
Amen.

Father of all,
I look back on what might have been.
I am also aware of what marvelous things
    have happened.
You told us to love our neighbors as ourselves.
Let me think of the good things that have happened
    to neighbors and friends.

Silence

Now allow me to reflect on the good things in my life.

Silence

Turn my mind to the needs of friends and neighbors,
    near and far.
How can I make a difference to their lives in your name?

Silence

And what should I do next, Lord, to do your will?

Silence

It's so important that I get started.
Thank you.
Amen.

Lord of connections,
our lives seem full of coincidences,
but perhaps we should think of them as God-incidences.
In looking back, help us to recall those marvelous
    moments
when chance meetings or events came together
    and led to amazing things.

Silence

And even where experiences were bad,
let us reflect on how we learned from the difficulties
and how we grew, even when we felt diminished.
We ask for your consolation in our regrets,
but also for your strength in our ability to console others
    in their regrets,
so that we can together be connected with the love
    of your Son, Jesus Christ.
Amen.

Consoling Lord,
watch over *N* at this time.
Comfort *her/his* distress and catch *her/his* tears.
May we be sensitive in looking back,
so that the reality of what has happened
is balanced by the positive memories of times past.
Help us to draw on the story of the New Testament
in acknowledging the past and embracing the future,
for our lives belong to those we love and those who
    love us,
including your Son, Jesus Christ.
Amen.

O God,
whose Son never looks back in anger,
let me always learn from his ways,
from Peter's spontaneity, but also his denials,
and from the other disciples as I recall their strengths
and weaknesses.

Silence

Then help me to appreciate all that Paul achieved
after his conversion.

Silence

May I remember the darkness as I light the candle,
but wonder at your creation in looking
   at what is revealed,
through your Son, Jesus Christ.
Amen.

Letting Go

Lord,
this house has been good to us.
We have seen the family grow up here.
We have played Scrabble in the living room,
and soccer in the back yard.
But now it is time to move on,
to say goodbye to this place
and wish the next owners well.
It will be in good hands,
and that's some consolation.
Through the one who is always our home,
your Son, Jesus Christ.
Amen.

God of every generation,
teach me how to let go of responsibilities
    that I have taken on:
not all of them, but when the time is right.
Help me to empower others, not seek to keep control,
even when I think I can do better, Lord!
Let me take your Son as a model of delegation
    and succession planning,
so that we grow stronger as a learning community.
Bring me the wisdom and the judgment to know
    when to let go and when to let be,
and may those who take over be blessed in their work,
    generous God.
Amen.

Almighty God,
create in our community a culture of developing
    each other's gifts,
recognizing talents as yet untapped,
seeing qualities yet to emerge
and accepting insights from different perspectives.
Where we can bring these on, let us do so;
where they need further development,
    may we encourage training;
and where they are ready to be tested,
make us ready to step aside and let people take
    responsibility
so that we can invest in the future—
ours and yours, Lord.
Amen.

Loving Lord,
as we remember what N meant to us,
we pray for those who mourn
and who, in their grief, are angry with you.
Comfort and console them, please, Lord,
as your Son showed his concern and love
for those who had lost a loved one.
We know that N is at peace with you now,
but help those who remain to know this
so that they can remember fondly,
but also go forward hopefully,
confident in the love of Jesus Christ.
Amen.

Father of all,
help me to acknowledge memories of things that have
    held me back;
in particular, Lord …
Can I leave these with you and let them go?
May the people I love and respect
show me a better way to move forward,
released from hate and hurt,
freed for work you want me to do
and strong in Christ.
Amen.

Giving Thanks

God of great gifts,
thank you for sharing all you have
so that we may see your great works
and enjoy the fruits of your creation.
As we immerse ourselves in the busyness of the world,
help us to look up and be grateful.
Help us to slow down and be glad.
Let us rejoice at what you have done
and give thanks where thanks are due,
remembering the gift of your Son, Jesus Christ.
Amen.

Heavenly Father,
I always come to you when I am in need,
but never when I should really thank you.
So let me mend my ways and honor your way
by giving grateful thanks for your loving kindness:
for all that makes up life in all its abundance;
for loved ones and fond memories;
for celebrations and future events;
for family and friends;
for favorite music and the arts of all kinds;
and for pets past and present.
Thank you, whose Son taught us to be grateful.
Amen.

God of grace,
we know that your gifts are made without condition;
so the freedom we have to choose
    is a gift beyond measure,
just as your creation gives infinite benefits.
However much we explore and however much
    we complain,
let us be both content and searching in the way we treat
    your world,
holding back where necessary and enjoying
    the abundance where appropriate.
Create in us a care for the environment
as if it were your home,
because we would be honored
if you would treat our home as always open to you too.
As Lord of the land and constant guest,
we wish to return your hospitality,
now and forever.
Amen.

Wonderful God,
thank you for all the friends we have,
for the fellowship and partnership they provide,
and for the sharing of joys and sorrows
that can bring both happiness and comfort.
We pray also for the friendless and rejected
in this country and many lands,
and ask that, through the love of your Son,
they may once again feel the warmth of friendship.
Help the agencies at work to restore
   the spirit of community,
to be strengthened and inspired to reconnect relationships and mend broken hearts.
We ask this in Jesus' name.
Amen.

Lord of our joys and fears,
let me reflect, as I give thanks . . .
for what I have learned . . .
for those who have taught me . . .
for those who have listened to me . . .
for how you have loved me . . .
for where I have visited . . .
for what I have achieved . . .
for future challenges . . .
for life itself . . .
Let me grow in faith and fortitude
as I grow older.
Let me be patient and kind
as I come closer to you,
long-suffering Lord.
Amen.

Facing Doubt

Forgiving Lord,
help me in this time of doubt:
doubt in myself; doubt in you;
doubt in every aspect of life just now.
It may seem strange that I still turn to you
when part of me feels that no one is listening.
If you are there, break through that veil of doubt
and show that all is not lost,
that you are there to support me,
you are there to inspire me,
and somewhere in me is the will to believe in you.
I doubt, therefore I am human,
but to believe would be very heaven.
Amen.

God of great faith,
look down on those of us who doubt
and help us to look up and see you.
We desperately want and need you,
but mostly pretend we can go it alone.
In times of trouble and torment
we are the first to ask you to sort things out,
just in case you can make a difference.
Then when everything is fine,
we tend not to thank you at all.
Give me some insight into the mind of our creator,
through Jesus Christ, our Lord.
Amen.

ONLY CONNECT

Long-suffering Lord of all,
help me to face my doubt and understand
    what form it takes as I reflect
on what I do believe in,
what I don't believe in,
how I came to have doubt,
how I would be convinced that there is more to faith
    than I imagine . . .
and how I might take steps
to "know thee more clearly,
love thee more dearly."*
Enlighten me and free me from doubt,
with the help of Christ.
Amen.

God of comfort,
you bring hope and health to the sick,
and even life to those near death.
Please console us in our doubts and difficulties
where faith is tested by worldly events
and when our Church is riven with disputes
    and disagreement.
Help me to hold on to the essence of faith,
rather than slide into doubt and despair
when the world is in a mess and your Church seems
    helpless to hope.
Bring me back to what Jesus would say and do,
and what he would call me to undertake for him
    and for you.
Then I might get back on the right track,
but only with the help of your Son, Jesus Christ.
Amen.

---

*Richard of Chichester, 1197–1253

All-seeing God,
you know my thoughts,
you know my doubts,
you know me.
Let me dare to reflect
on your thoughts about the world . . .
on your doubts about mankind . . .
on your doubts about me . . .
Then tell me your hopes and dreams
for the future of your Church in the world . . .
for the future of our planet . . .
for my future and the future of my family . . .
Thank you for helping me to face my doubts
and for sharing your hopes and plans,
which your Son died to show us.
Amen.

Having Faith

God of revelation,
in all the trials and tribulations I have experienced
 recently,
the only thing that has kept me going is faith in you.
Strengthen my resolve to keep the faith,
even when it seems that all is lost.
Give me a sense of your Son's purpose,
as he carried out your mission to bring us back to you.
In all my difficulties, keep me focused on his resolve
 to do your will.
Let me learn my lesson and take my cue
 from his great task,
and play my humble part in your grand design,
with the help of your Son, Jesus Christ.
Amen.

Merciful Lord,
look favorably on *N*
as troubles mount and *his/her* faith is tested.
You inspired that faith in *him/her*, and *he/she* needs your
    comfort now.
I pray that *he/she* turns to you and seeks your help.
May *he/she* find that assistance through family
    and friends and through the family network.
Most of all, may *he/she* feel your presence
at *his/her* side,
in *his/her* heart,
in *his/her* prayers,
in *his/her* sleeping,
in *his/her* waking,
and in the church where *he/she* feels at home.
Through your Son who has never ceased to love,
    Jesus Christ.
Amen.

Rock of our lives,
you are the cornerstone of our faith
and the mainstay of our hearts.
Help us to grow in our desire to know you better.
Make us search and search again
to understand the full extent of your love for us,
so that when we face the changes and chances of life
we are able to turn to you with confidence of
    consolation.
As we pray for your hopes to be fulfilled,
may we seek to meet the challenges you set us,
through the help of your Son, Jesus Christ.
Amen.

Heavenly Father,
give us a glimpse of heaven
in the smile of others and the faith of saints.
Give us a sound of eternity
in the stillness of waters and the beauty of music.
Give us a sign of transcendence
in the soaring of a spire and the starkness of the cross.
Give us hope for the future
in the cry of a baby and a school bell sounding.
Give us a clue to the right way
in a prayer answered and a Bible passage understood.
Give us a true appreciation of your generosity
in giving us your Son, our Savior, Jesus Christ.
Amen.

Lord of beginnings and endings,
you brought us hope at the first.
Bring us faith at the last.
You created in us a desire to know and love you.
Bring us a desire to worship you in word and song.
Let every new step bring a fresh experience.
Let every new convert bring joy to us all.
Let every new day be greeted with thanks.
And while evenings are to be savored,
our nighttimes full of peace and rest,
so we pray that there is always a new dawn,
whether in this world or the next.
We ask this through the one who brought us the fruits
    of a new heaven and earth,
your Son, Jesus Christ.
Amen.

www.ingramcontent.com/pod-product-compliance
Lightning Source LLC
Chambersburg PA
CBHW052211090526
44584CB00019BA/3050